The
Love and Sex Life
of an
Aromantic Asexual

--By Laurel Federbush

This book is part of me, so it's dedicated to someone.

Yes, the name of this book is intended as an oxymoron...but not entirely. Would it also be an oxymoron to describe something as an oxymoron that's true?

I recently found out that I was an aromantic asexual. Well, I sort of knew that all my life, but I didn't know there was a name for it, that it was a legitimate sexual orientation, or that there were lots of others like me.

I basically just thought I was damaged, dysfunctional, and abnormal.

First to define the terms:

An asexual is someone who doesn't feel sexually attracted to anyone, and has no desire to have sex.

An aromantic asexual is someone who doesn't even experience the kind of love that would lead to sex.

There's very little written about aromantic asexuality, or about any kind of asexuality, for that matter. So I just thought I'd add what I know about the subject based entirely on my own life, my feelings and experiences.

The more of us who get our stories out there, the better off we'll all be, and the better-understood this particular type of sexual identity will be.

LOVE

Being in love for me is probably what most people would label as hero worship. It's sort of like having my own personal guru (who never signed up for the job), although I'm not into eastern mysticism, so I don't know how accurate the comparison is.

A couple of my family members who weren't aromantic or asexual had a similar love style, although not exclusively—they were also able to live conventional married lives. So I don't know if this love style is unique to or even typical of aromantic asexuals, but it's the only kind of love I know.

Tried to do things more conventionally, but it never even came close to happening for me. And my crushes completely overwhelm me.

If I love you, it's because you're awesome. I mean that literally: I'm totally and completely in awe of you. It doesn't mean I can't see that you have flaws, or I expect you to be unnaturally perfect. It's just that your flaws are part of your natural perfection.

So, in other words, I get intense crushes. Not meaning that I picture having sex with or marrying the object of my affection. My "crush" is someone I look up to, someone I really admire. A protective figure. Someone who is way, way out of my league.

I'm attracted to someone's energy. Someone who radiates an energy that I can actually feel, and that feels beautiful to me. I want to immerse myself in that person's energy, take it into myself, let it surround and purify me.

But it's not a possessive kind of thing. If you have a wife or girlfriend, I love her, too. Your kids are the best! And if you have a dog, I love your dog (or cat, or guinea pig...).

I never understood the thing about not wanting to be "just friends." I'd love to be your friend! There is no greater honor in the world.

SEXUALITY

I'm not entirely comfortable talking about love and sexuality in the same book. That's because my style of love doesn't lead to sex. And lots of things about my sexuality are embarrassing to me. But since I'm explaining what being an aromantic asexual means to me, here goes...

Maybe you have the misconception, as I did before, that being an asexual means not having any sexual feelings. It doesn't. It simply means someone doesn't want to have sex with anyone.

Which brings up the next question people have: If you don't want to have sex with people, then what?

To save anyone the trouble of speculating, I would like to talk about the type of things an asexual might fanaticize about. Specifically, the type of things I fanaticize about. They may or may not be representative of anyone else.

(I don't think my fantasies are typical of non-asexuals, because if they were, erotic movies and pornography would be way, way different.)

My fantasies are all variations on a central theme, namely, being treated like an inanimate object. People often talk about women being used as sex objects, but that's not the same thing. A "sex object" in that context means a very attractive woman who is willing to have sex, not an inanimate object.

It may seem paradoxical that the idea of being treated like an inanimate object (a useful one) would be sexually arousing, but to me it is. Perhaps this is true of some other asexuals, or maybe even some people who don't identify that way. Or maybe it's just one of my personal quirks.

I'll list a few of my fantasies here, just to give you a picture of what I mean, but hopefully not enough to thoroughly repulse you:

being bought and sold, or given as a gift;

being owned;

being used as a piece of furniture;

being referred to as "it";

being decorated and
displayed like a statue;

being used as a canvas for someone to paint…

...maybe you get the idea.

There is one way that love and sexuality are related for me, and it's this:

the idea of being dedicated to someone and being something good in that person's life is a real turn-on. That's probably the best thing about my kind of sexuality—the asexual kind.

So, that's where I am, as an aromantic asexual.

That's me.

If you would like more information on the subject of aromantic asexuality, or asexuality in general, here are a few good sources:

"Asexual and Happy," by Kim Kaletsky, The New York Times "Modern Love" (July 2, 2015);

The Asexual Visibility and Education Network, www.asexuality.org;

Facebook groups: "Aromantic Asexuals," "Aromantic Talk," "Asexuality"

www.ingramcontent.com/pod-product-compliance
Lightning Source LLC
Chambersburg PA
CBHW060344290526
45791CB00004B/1523